AF415671

NATURALLY YOUNG

Anti-aging methods and tips

INDEX

Introduction

Everyone has heard the old adage "age is only a number" and for many aspects of life this is still true. Remember, you are only as old as you feel. Still, it is a little difficult to assimilate what we see once we get in front of the mirror, especially if we don't like what we see. Keep in mind that this will require some sacrifice on your part and you should learn to accept this sacrifice and the changes it will bring.

For many years, many scientists, doctors and beauticians have struggled to figure out the secret to looking young forever. The truth is that staying young forever is simply impossible.

But there are things we can do to slow down the aging process. There is no need to spend thousands and thousands of dollars on expensive treatments or risky surgeries. But by following these tips you will find yourself feeling and looking young again with simple health tips that will help improve your overall health.

I hope you enjoy reading this book and we hope it will help you feel and look better!

Chapter 1: Habits That Will Improve How You Feel and Look

Exercising regularly

Believe it or not, one of the most important things we can do to improve our appearance and how we look when we are a little older is to exercise. A recent study by the American College of Sports Medicine found that exercise is one of the best ways to improve mobility as we age. When I say exercise, I don't necessarily mean a weight-lifting session or a half-marathon. Simple things like a brisk 15-minute walk or a yoga class can go a long way. By improving mobility we will not only feel younger, but we will improve in

several aspects of our life that test our body's potential.

Things like climbing a flight of stairs or bending down to pick up the newspaper are things that can be a challenge for some people, but as long as you stay in shape, they shouldn't become a problem over time.

Getting enough sleep

If you're like most adults, you probably don't get enough sleep every day to fully recover after a long day. Believe it or not, it is possible that your lack of adequate sleep may be causing you to gain weight. Instead of focusing on getting a good night's sleep, we concentrate on getting our energy from a cup of coffee or sugary treats, which eventually leads to weight gain. This also means that because you're tired, you probably don't have

time to cook a healthy meal, so you'll go out and eat some fast food after work and end up eating a million calories. It's a vicious cycle that ultimately leads to lower activity levels and higher calorie intake. It's natural for our brains to respond to lack of sleep by going for comfort foods, but what is the immediate result of this? Yes, you can stay awake, but at what cost? Unwanted fat, moodiness, tiredness, irritability and other symptoms.

It's no secret that our bodies heal themselves when we sleep. By allowing our bodies to reach a state of deep sleep we are giving our bodies a chance to recover from all the things we have put them through during the day.

When we sleep, we allow the cells in our face to produce collagen, a fibrous tissue in our body that is a key ingredient for firm, youthful-looking skin. The recommended amount of sleep an adult should get varies between 7.5 and 8 hours of continuous sleep. Remember that sleep debt is like credit card debt, if you keep accumulating debt you will eventually go bankrupt.

To get a good night's sleep you need to create the perfect environment that promotes healthy sleep.

One of the first things I recommend is to get rid of the TV in your room, you need to relax before going to bed and by watching TV in our bed we are letting our brains get excited until they fall out.

Get rid of the smartphone too. You can do some light reading under a night light, but that's it. Don't eat heavy meals or caffeinated drinks before bed either, as this will cause your digestive system to work overtime and can affect your sleep.

Quitting smoking

Smoking is undoubtedly one of the worst habits you can acquire, especially if you try to stay young. Cigarette smoking has been shown to accelerate the aging process of our cells and has been shown to accelerate the aging process in people as young as 20. Cigarettes contain over 5000 ingredients that when smoked are converted into unpleasant chemical compounds that can affect the composition of the skin, as well as the teeth, fingers, lungs, mouth, tongue, eyes and immune system. Smoking also affects the skin on the face, reducing the amount of blood the skin receives, which can lead to wrinkling and staining of the skin.

Quitting smoking can be one of the hardest things to do. Fortunately, there are many alternatives for people who are trying to quit smoking. But if one of your priorities is to stay young, quitting smoking will give you almost immediate results and I guarantee that you will start feeling better almost immediately.

Protect yourself from the sun

You may already know how dangerous UV radiation is to your skin, but a recent study concluded through micro topography that people who do not wear sunscreen or sunglasses showed damage to deeper skin, elastic fibers and collagen. And patients who did use sunscreen showed up to 24% less damage to their skin.

By exposing our skin to constant UV radiation from the sun, we are prematurely damaging our skin and slowing down the regenerative process that takes place in our skin cells. Not only that, but constant UV radiation has been scientifically linked to terrible conditions such as skin cancer, melanoma, premature aging and other skin damage.

This is not unique to the face, but the skin on our forearms, hands, neck and shoulders can easily be affected by prolonged exposure to UV radiation.

Avoid stress

Stressful situations and general anxiety have a very stressful effect on your body. The work-related exhaustion associated with high levels of stress affects the DNA of the skin cells by shortening the telomeres, causing the cells to become damaged or even die.

Not only that, but even the idea of being stressed can increase the risk of age-related disorders, causing the brain to go into overdrive. A recent study showed that an increased stress load could lead the human brain into age-related symptoms.

It is very important that we learn to manage stress and anxiety situations by calming down and adapting to these situations. Experts recommend that we allow ourselves periods of deep meditation and relaxation. Identifying the sources of stress in your life can also go a long way toward improving your overall mental health. Look at your habits and attitudes and accept responsibility for your actions.

If the stress becomes unbearable, it may be a good idea to seek professional help. If all else fails, think about taking a day off, sometimes this helps a lot in dealing with stress, but don't spend all day in bed thinking about how horrible tomorrow is going to be, plan your day ahead, make sure you plan around eating a healthy and satisfying meal and getting some light exercise like a brisk walk, bike ride, or swim.

Maybe even take the dog for a walk! The plan here is to take a break from the many things we have to do every day. By "readjusting" our bodies and minds we can easily overcome the effects of stress.

Chapter 2: Your Diet and Aging

While having good, healthy habits is a great way to stay young, it's also important to remember that a good diet is good for you.

From brain to bone, what we eat ends up playing a big part in how well we age.

By eating the right foods we can make our bodies and minds healthier and able to perform longer, avoiding injuries and poor skin appearance. Here is a list of foods that are recommended to slow down the aging process in our bodies

Fruits and vegetables

One of the cornerstones of our diet and one that we often neglect. The colorful fruits and vegetables are full of antioxidants. I'm sure you've heard this term before, but what exactly are antioxidants? Antioxidants are chemical compounds found in foods and supplements that are able to slow down the normal effects of oxidation on tissues. We need to remember that this process, even though it damages the skin and other tissues, is completely normal. There is no way to stop it, but we can slow it down by eating foods such as fruits and vegetables.

By eating foods rich in vitamin C, zinc and beta-carotene we can preserve our vision by preventing eye degeneration, one of the major causes of blindness in older adults.

Leafy vegetables such as spinach and kale and other colorful produce such as corn, oranges and melon are full of these three vital antioxidants.

If you're a wine lover, you'll also be happy to know that a common antioxidant found in red grapes like wine, called resveratrol, is a fantastic antioxidant that protects the body against cancer- and heart-related damage, reducing inflammation and preventing the oxidation of cholesterol. In short, if you want to have a glass of red wine once in a while, then do so.

Fish

Fish is absolutely full of Omega-3 fatty acids that offer fantastic anti-aging benefits. Omega-3s are not only vital for our bodies, but they also help our bodies reduce high cholesterol levels, which puts us at risk for heart disease. Omega-3 acids specifically (EPA and DHA) can also help improve joint conditions and help relieve joint stiffness, which will definitely make you feel younger again.

Finally, some Omega-3s may help moderately to elevate your mood and interact with some antidepressants to enhance their effects.

Normally, it is always a good idea to try to get your Omega-3s from natural food sources, supplements are fine too, but the absorption rate is significantly higher when obtained from natural sources. Some of the fish varieties that contain high levels of Omega-3 fatty acids are anchovies, herring, mackerel, salmon (try to get wild fish if possible), tuna and trout.

Dairy

I have noticed a recent thread in food health where dairy is demonized for its high levels of fat, hormones and the effect it causes on the digestive system of certain people.

I'm not sure why this dairy war has gained so much popularity, but I'm very concerned because most dairy products are fantastic. The calcium and vitamin D found in milk, cheese and yogurt play a vital role in keeping our bones strong and preventing osteoporosis.

Choosing low-fat dairy products will also help keep cholesterol levels low, reducing the chances of heart disease, stroke and more. If you have legitimate lactose intolerance (another term I see widely used) you can try to find dairy products that are lactose free but fortified with calcium and vitamin D.

Nuts

All types of nuts (as long as they are unsalted) have incredible anti-aging effects. Walnuts, almonds, cashews and pecans are excellent whether they are eaten alone or added to other foods on this list, such as salads or yoghurts.

Nuts have high levels of Omega-3 acids and are rich in monounsaturated fats (one of the so-called "good" fats) that help improve the condition of the heart. Overall, a portion of 10-15 unsalted nuts every day will give you excellent health benefits without adding a significant amount of calories to your calorie intake.

Tea

Tea is usually full of antioxidants, but if you really want to go the extra mile, drink green or black tea. Green and black teas have 10 times the amount of antioxidants found in fruits and vegetables.

Green and black teas come from the same plant. Camellia Sinesis, which is rich in polyphenols, an antioxidant that helps detoxify our skin cells and other tissues. This plant also has many epicatechins and catechins.

Two of the most important antioxidants for the body because they help reduce toxins related to atherosclerosis and cancer.

Berries

Berries are well known for their anti-aging properties as they contain flavonoids, powerful antioxidants that protect the body from free radicals and aging.

The good thing about berries is that there are many different ways to eat them, mix them into yogurt or cereals, freeze them and mix them into tasty shakes, or eat them alone, dry or fresh. Berries are also available all year round and are quite cheap. Consider buying them in bulk and freezing them if necessary.

Studies show that one cup of mixed berries a day provides all the antioxidants you need in one day. However, I recommend that you get your antioxidants from different food sources and supplements as it may be easier for your body to absorb them.

Chapter 3: Foods to Avoid

Believe it or not, it is quite possible that your diet will make you old or prevent you from making anti-aging efforts. What you put on your plate will ultimately determine how quickly you age and how quickly these symptoms of aging manifest themselves in your body. By eating poor quality foods like refined sugars and simple carbohydrates, you will end up damaging the collagen in your skin, making you look tired and old over time.

Foods such as trans fats have also been shown to cause inflammation and constipation, which will affect the health of your digestive, nervous and circulatory systems by trapping toxins in your gastrointestinal tract, kidneys and blood.

It may also be a good idea to limit the amount of fried or battered foods you eat. Anything that has been fried will cause inflammation throughout your body.

Be especially careful with foods that are high in trans fats, as they will raise cholesterol and lower good cholesterol. As always, be sure to check your food labels for any warning signs. If you are not completely convinced, it may be a good idea to abstain.

Chapter 4: Cosmetic products and natural remedies

One of the advantages of living in these modern times is the large number of beauty products we have access to. From moisturizers to exfoliants, to deep cleansers, to night creams... But do we really need all these products? What are some of the natural products that can be made at home at a low price? What kind of cream is right for you? Moisturizers and night creams that cost hundreds and hundreds of dollars and come wrapped in luxurious packaging are fine don't get me wrong, but why should you spend so much money on a product that can be easily replaced? Moisturizers do the same thing, they simply seal in the moisture in your skin. But let's take a look at what these products do and how they can be easily replaced.

Cleansers

The basic purpose of cleansers is to cleanse the skin. Most cleansers have an active time of 10 seconds or less, and most dermatologists agree that any product that stays on your face for just 10 seconds won't really do much for your skin. Yes, you can spend a lot of money on a French-made cleanser and it will definitely do its job very well. But if you ask any dermatologist he'll tell you he only uses a basic $5 cleanser that you can get at your local pharmacy. By removing dirt, oil, makeup, and other toxins from your skin, you can improve the overall health of your skin and make sure that bacteria and other harmful particles are kept away. Since facial cleansers do a much better

job of deep cleansing the skin than a regular bar of soap, it is vital to keep a facial cleanser in your beauty products. Always remember to wash your hands before applying the cleanser and then splash your face with warm water. Rub some cleanser on your hands and rub your face up to your neck. Rinse your skin with cold water and dry your face with a clean towel or cloth.

Moisturizers

As stated earlier, the job of moisturizers is to keep the skin hydrated by sealing in moisture. Moisturizers are usually made from a combination of oils, creams, and plant extracts and can be used on the face and body. Moisturizers are often enriched with vitamins and other nutrients. Once a moisturizer is applied to the skin, it is instantly absorbed and begins its job of replenishing the skin's moisture, vitamins, and minerals to keep the skin elastic, smooth, and wrinkle-free. It is very important that you choose the right moisturizer for your skin, whether it is dry or oily, and also remember to choose a thicker moisturizer for the winter if you live in an area where it is cold. The best time of day to apply moisturizer to your face is right after your shower, usually within 5 minutes of turning the water on, as we want to attract as much moisture as possible. Remember to use a gentle touch and do not pull on your skin.

Apply the moisturizer to your face at least twice a day; in the morning and at night. One last piece of advice, people who have skin conditions such as rashes or acne will usually want to skip the moisturizer because they think that adding an oily product to their skin will make the condition worse.

This couldn't be further from the truth, damaged skin needs as much moisture as it can get, and by using a moisturizer we are providing a healthy skin environment that will speed up the healing process.

Neck Cream

Our necks are one of the places on our bodies most likely to get wrinkles. Whether from constant exposure to the elements, stretching or lack of collagen, our necks tend to become a problem area. By choosing a good neck cream, depending on the type of skin you have, we can ensure that our necks stay wrinkle-free. Remember to apply the night cream after exfoliating to the upper chest, removing the layer of dead skin that will allow the active ingredients of the cream to be absorbed by the skin more quickly. If possible, look for a neck cream that has Retinol; an animal form of vitamin A, which

is essential for skin health. Another ingredient to consider is peptides, as they help the production of collagen in our system and improve the elasticity of the skin on our necks, chest and face.

Finally, creams with Niacin, are able to penetrate the skin barrier and strengthen the skin, making it more flexible and less prone to wrinkle over time. Neck creams with these ingredients have been shown to dramatically improve not only the texture, but also the tone and firmness of the neck and surrounding areas.

Sunscreen

Sunscreen is the only product that will prevent your skin from aging naturally. When choosing a brand of sunscreen, consider all the options available. Does the sunscreen protect against UV rays? Is it sweat and water resistant? Is it fragrant? Is it chalky or oily? Choose a sunscreen that you are comfortable with and make sure it has an SPF of at least 50. Put it on at least 20 minutes before you go out and make sure your skin is dry and clean before you put it on.

If you know in advance that you will be spending a lot of time in the sun, consider wearing a hat and try to stay in the shade as much as possible by gliding around in the sun. Remember that the best sunscreen is the one that works for you, find a texture that you like and don't forget to apply the sunscreen to all areas of your body that will be exposed to direct sunlight; your ears, neck, shoulders, hands, arms and legs can easily get sunburned and we tend to ignore those parts of our body because we focus too much on the face.

Exfoliants

Exfoliating your skin is one of the best things you can do to make sure you look young for a long time. Our skin cells will naturally shed millions and millions of skin cells every day. When this natural shedding slows down or stops due to dry skin damage, the sun or other conditions, our skin will tend to look dry and flaky with spots and blemishes.

Using an exfoliant we can help our skin rejuvenate faster because once we get rid of the dead skin layers, our skin will look immediately bright and full of life while improving its long-term flexibility. I normally recommend exfoliating no more than once a day, just before bed, as this is when our faces accumulate the most dead skin cells.

You can start by splashing your face with cold water and slowly rubbing the exfoliant all over your face, hands and neck. Let it sit on your skin for at least 2 or 3 minutes and rinse with cold water. Dry your face with a clean towel and when you are done you can go ahead and apply any other product you wish, such as foundation, night cream or sunscreen.

Chapter 5: Supplements

Living in these modern times, it can be very difficult to get all the nutrients from our foods. We live in times when eating well has become a chore and we have been driven by the comfort of eating poorly.

While it is always a good idea to get nutrients directly from food, I realize that this is not always possible, and that is where supplements come in.

Supplements will help us absorb all the nutrients our bodies need to look and feel young, and while they are not necessary, they are always a good help when it comes to staying young.

Calcium

Calcium is a mineral found in several foods such as dairy products and works together with vitamin D to provide the nutrients needed to create a healthy environment for burning fat.

Calcium is normally stored in fat cells and recent studies have found that the more calcium a fat cell has, the more fat that cell will burn in the long run. Calcium also helps reduce the rate of fat absorption in the gastrointestinal tract, reducing the amount of excess fat the body stores from fatty foods.

Glucomannan Extract

Glucomannan extract is obtained from a South Asian plant called Konjac, which has a high fiber content and is considered very effective for diabetes and glucose control, but also offers weight loss properties.

This plant has been an important food source for Asians for many years and its high levels of fiber help absorb water in the gastrointestinal tract, reducing the absorption of complex carbohydrates and cholesterol and has been used for many years as a folk remedy for obesity.

B-Complex

By obtaining a vitamin from the B-Complex you get the full range of B-vitamins, including B1, B2, B3, B5, B6, B7, B9 and B12. Keep in mind that unless you have a significant deficiency in the B vitamins, you should limit the amount of B supplements you take.

By far the most important of these is B12, which helps raise energy levels and increases the rate of metabolism in your body, aiding in weight loss and fat absorption.

Coenzyme Q10

Without a doubt, one of the best supplements you can get for anti-aging. Normally our bodies produce this coenzyme naturally. Q10 helps our bodies produce ATP or adenosine triphosphate, which is the fuel that helps our cells function. However, as we age, our bodies produce less and less of this coenzyme, resulting in some diseases such as Parkinson's, cancer and heart disease.

A recent study has shown that taking Q10 as a supplement reduces the risk of heart disease and promotes the absorption of antioxidants into the bloodstream. Q10 has also been shown to keep sugar levels in our body low, as well as cholesterol.

If you decide to take the supplement, keep in mind that it comes in various forms, from capsules to tablets. I would recommend getting them in gel form if possible, as our bodies absorb them faster than capsules.

Aspirin

Believe it or not, one of the best supplements you can take to slow down the effects of time could be in your bathroom! Aspirin not only eliminates headache, but is also excellent for relieving mild pain and increasing blood flow, which is one of the best things it can do to improve your overall health, as it will repair cells, improve circulation, improve

kidney and liver function, and reduce the risk of heart disease and colon cancer by delaying the development of polyps and other toxins. However, don't go overboard with aspirin, as increased doses have been linked to abdominal pain and diarrhea.

Carnitine

Carnitine is a natural nutrient produced in the liver and is responsible for converting fat reserves into energy. Carnitine has also been shown to reduce the symptoms of angina by increasing overall circulation and reducing joint pain. Carnitine has also been shown to reduce the risk of Alzheimer's disease and improve long-term memory, as well as help the development of other mental conditions such as dementia or depression. Men will also be happy to know that carnitine increases sperm counts and has been linked to increased testosterone levels. I recommend

taking at least 1 gram of carnitine per day and up to 3 grams for patients suffering from poor circulation.

Human growth hormone

This is a sensitive issue since most people associate human growth hormone (HGH) with professional bodybuilders or athletes. First of all, HGH is produced naturally in the body by the pituitary gland, and although it is vital in early development, HGH can greatly help us decrease the time in our bodies and help us reverse the effects of aging.

Synthetic HGH has been available since the mid-1980s and although no official studies have proven the effects of HGH, this hormone is still used by thousands of people to heal faster, promote bone density growth and increase testosterone levels. I encourage anyone considering HGH as a treatment to consult with their doctor before making any drastic decisions.

Conclusion

Aging is a fact of life, whether we like it or not, our bodies will eventually age and decompose. What we can do is lessen the effects of time on our bodies by following some simple tips that will help us improve how we look and feel.

Remember that if we eat right, exercise and change our habits a little, we can greatly improve our quality of life and how we feel about ourselves.

Of course it is possible to stay young longer by using expensive products and getting risky surgeries. But why should we let it get to that point when everything we need is within our reach? By naturally improving our body conditions we are not only extending its life, but we are also taking control of how time and the environment will affect us.

The media, peer pressure, and other factors have changed the way we see ourselves, and if we want to conform to those standards while staying healthy, we have to follow habits that improve the way we feel and look.

It is amazing to think that around the end of the last century, life expectancy was less than 50 years for most first world nations and it is amazing how much life has changed in the last 100 years or so where life expectancy is approaching the mid-1970s.

This not only proves that the science of anti-aging works, but also that the conditions in